Jr. Graphic Mythologies™

CHINESE MYTHOLOGY

The Four Dragons

Tom Daning

PowerKiDS
press

New York

Published in 2007 by The Rosen Publishing Group, Inc.
29 East 21st Street, New York, NY 10010

First Edition

Editors: Julia Wong and Daryl Heller
Book Design: Greg Tucker
Illustrations: Q2A

Library of Congress Cataloging-in-Publication Data

Daning, Tom.
  Chinese mythology : the four dragons / by Tom Daning.— 1st ed.
      p. cm. — (Jr. graphic mythologies)
  Includes index.
  ISBN (10) 1-4042-3400-4 (13) 978-1-4042-3400-0 (lib. bdg.) —
ISBN (10) 1-4042-2153-0 (13) 978-1-4042-2153-6 (pbk.)
  1. Mythology, Chinese—Juvenile literature. 2. Legends—China. 3. Folklores—China.
I. Title. II. Series.
  BL1825.D35 2007
  398.20931'0454—dc22
                                      2006002787

Manufactured in the United States of America

CONTENTS

MAJOR CHARACTERS

Long-wang *is the Chinese name for all the dragons. The dragons were in charge of all the water in the world. Yellow Dragon, Long Dragon, Pearl Dragon, and Black Dragon were four of the Long-wang.*

The Jade Emperor *(Yu Huang) was the ruler of the whole world. All the other gods worked for the Jade Emperor.*

The god of the sea *(Yi-qiang) was also the god of the wind. When he was in the water, he turned into a fish and rode two dragons. When he was in the air, he turned into a bird.*

The god of the mountain *(Tai-yue Da-di) was in charge of Earth and all people. He kept track of every person on Earth. He kept a record of when they were born and when they died.*

THE FOUR DRAGONS

LONG AGO THERE WERE NO RIVERS IN CHINA. THE SALTY SEA WAS THE ONLY WATER.

YELLOW, PEARL, BLACK, AND LONG, TOGETHER WE SING OUR DRAGON SONG!

MERRILY DANCING, WILD AND FREE, WE LIVE OUR LIVES UPON THE SEA!

IN THE SEA LIVED FOUR **CAREFREE** DRAGONS. THEY WERE YELLOW DRAGON, PEARL DRAGON, BLACK DRAGON, AND LONG DRAGON.

ONE DAY THE DRAGONS DECIDED TO HAVE SOME FUN IN THE SKY.

EIGHTEEN, NINETEEN, TWENTY! READY OR NOT, HERE I COME!

WHEN PEARL DRAGON OPENED HIS EYES, HE SAW A TERRIBLE SIGHT.

LOOK!

THE PEOPLE WERE PRAYING BECAUSE IT HAD NOT RAINED IN MANY MONTHS.

THE PEOPLE WERE HUNGRY AND THIRSTY. THEY HAD NO WATER TO DRINK.

THE CROPS COULD NOT GROW. THE PEOPLE HAD NO FOOD TO EAT.

THE ANIMALS WERE DYING AS WELL.

SO THE KINDHEARTED DRAGONS TRAVELED FAR ABOVE THE CLOUDS TO THE PALACE OF THE MIGHTY JADE EMPEROR.

WONDERFUL!

GOOD THINKING, LONG DRAGON!

EXCELLENT!

I'M AFRAID THAT THE JADE EMPEROR WILL BE VERY ANGRY WITH US, THOUGH.

WE DON'T CARE IF HE IS ANGRY! THE PEOPLE NEED HELP!

THE DRAGONS FILLED THEIR MOUTHS WITH SEAWATER.

THE DRAGONS WORKED HARD. THEY WATERED EVERY CLOUD IN THE SKY.

THE CLOUDS WERE FULL OF WATER. AT LAST IT BEGAN TO RAIN.

15

WHEN THE RAIN FELL, THE PEOPLE HAD WATER TO DRINK.

THE CROPS BEGAN TO GROW AGAIN.
THE PEOPLE WOULD BE ABLE TO EAT.

THE ANIMALS BECAME HEALTHY AGAIN.

ALL THE PEOPLE IN THE VILLAGE
WERE **GRATEFUL** FOR THE RAIN.

THE DRAGONS **CELEBRATED**. HOWEVER, THEY DID NOT KNOW THAT THE GOD OF THE SEA WAS WATCHING THEM.

THE GOD OF THE SEA TOLD THE JADE EMPEROR WHAT THE DRAGONS HAD DONE.

FOOLS! I WILL TEACH THEM NOT TO **MEDDLE** IN MY BUSINESS!

THE JADE EMPEROR CALLED FOR HIS ARMY.

GO, GENERAL! ARREST THE FOUR DRAGONS!

THE FOUR DRAGONS WERE STUCK INSIDE FOUR MOUNTAINS.

THE DRAGONS DID NOT FORGET THE PEOPLE, THOUGH.

THE DRAGONS TURNED THEMSELVES INTO RIVERS THAT SPLASHED DOWN THE SIDES OF THE MOUNTAINS.

THE RIVERS FLOWED THROUGH THE VILLAGES. THEY WOULD BRING THE PEOPLE WATER FOREVER.

FINALLY THE RIVERS RAN INTO THE SEA. THE DRAGONS WERE HOME AGAIN.

FAMILY TREE

Jade Emperor
Yu Huang
Ruler of the Universe

God of the Mountain
Tai-yue Da-di
Ruler of Earth and People

Dragons
Long-wang
Rulers of All Water

God of the Sea
Yi-qiang
Ruler of the Sea and the Wind

Black Dragon
Heilongjiang River

Yellow Dragon
Huang He River

Long Dragon
Zhujiang River

Pearl Dragon
Yangtze River

GLOSSARY

carefree (KER-free) Free from care or worry.

celebrated (SEH-luh-brayt-ed) Observed an important occasion with special activities.

eternity (ih-TUR-nuh-tee) Forever.

grateful (GRAYT-ful) Thankful.

humble (HUM-bul) Low in rank or status.

intrusion (in-TROO-zhun) An unwanted visit.

majesty (MAH-juh-stee) A word used to address a king or ruler.

meddle (MEH-del) To interest oneself in what is not one's concern.

merciful (MER-sih-ful) Showing or having kindness, loving.

proclaim (proh-KLAYM) To state.

punish (PUH-nish) To cause someone pain or loss for a crime he or she has committed.

sacrifice (SA-kruh-fys) Something that has been given up for a belief.

scoop (SKOOP) To pick up as if with a spoon or shovel.

INDEX

WEB SITES

Due to the changing nature of Internet links, Powerkids Press has developed an online list of Web sites related to the subject of this book. This site is updated regularly. Please use this link to access the list:
www.powerkidslinks.com/myth/dragons/